SUMANA ROY is the author of *How I Became a Tree* and *Missing: A Novel.* She writes from Siliguri, India.

ALSO BY SUMANA ROY

How I Became a Tree (2017)
Missing: A Novel (2018)

Out of Syllabus

poems

Sumana Roy

SPEAKING TIGER PUBLISHING PVT. LTD
4381/4, Ansari Road, Daryaganj
New Delhi 110002

Copyright © Sumana Roy 2019

First published in paperback by Speaking Tiger 2019

ISBN: 978-93-88874-60-1
eISBN: 978-93-88874-32-8

10 9 8 7 6 5 4 3 2 1

Typeset in Goudy Old Style by SÜRYA, New Delhi

All rights reserved.
No part of this publication may be reproduced, transmitted, or stored in
a retrieval system, in any form or by any means, electronic,
mechanical, photocopying, recording or otherwise,
without the prior permission of the publisher.

This book is sold subject to the condition that it shall not,
by way of trade or otherwise, be lent, resold, hired out, or otherwise
circulated, without the publisher's prior consent, in any
form of binding or cover other than
that in which it is published.

*If Galileo had said in verse that the world moved,
the Inquisition might have let him alone.*
—Thomas Hardy

CONTENTS

MATHEMATICS

    The Third Is a Betrayal   3
    Singular-Plural   5

HISTORY

    Dancing Girl, Mohenjodaro   9

CHEMISTRY

    Elements in the Periodic Table   13

BIOLOGY

    Illness in Instalments   17
    Touch   22

NATURAL SCIENCE

    Rain   27
    Umbrella   30

PHYSICS

    'Are You Lonesome Tonight?'   35
    Biraha   37
    Long-distance Relationship   39

GEOGRAPHY

    Nicosia   43
    Death by Darjeeling   48
    Finding Light in Sukna   50
    Night by the Torsha   52

HOME SCIENCE

House   57
'Good Housekeeping'   64
Chair   65

GENERAL KNOWLEDGE

Sunlight   71
'Every Girl Is Dinner'   73

PHILOSOPHY

Marriage in Hostage   77
Silent Night, Holy Night   78
Secrets   80

EDUCATION

Shanti: Niketans   83

MORAL SCIENCE

Adult   93
Lust   94
Sadness   97

SECOND LANGUAGE

My Nephew Grows into Verbs   101
Mirik: Travelling with Uncommon Nouns   103
The Lexicographer in Lower Assam   107
Spit Feast   109
'Go to Pakistan'   111
Sounds   114

BOTANY

The Afterlife of Trees and Their Lovers   119

ART

Portraits: Shards   125

Mathematics

*The proper numbers march together
 their uniforms button bright;
 the rational numbers walk alone.*

—Linda Pastan

The Third Is a Betrayal

Who is the third who walks always beside you?
When I count, there are only you and I together
But when I look up the white road
There is always another one walking beside you
... But who is that on the other side of you?
—T. S. Eliot, 'The Waste Land'

Marriage, you once said, was a comedy of manners,
and only that. It's the way you rest the fork on
your breakfast plate: an embalmed gesture
of a lifetime, like yawning is to boredom.

I disagreed again.

It's the steam from the teacup—
only cold will give birth to the display of heat.
And so anger and vapour: now both lost lottery tickets.

Not scarlet but egg-yolk yellow—the colour of overdose,
of gluttony, of blind-lane travelogues in middle age.
Of adultery.
There's a stranger in that word. And a train whistle.

Adultery became a street lamp: my nights stayed up with them.
Everything became eating: the marriage a fish;
we took turns to sort out bones. The sea was elsewhere.
We spoke to each other in the mirror—mediated by a third,
not noticing the gaps between seeing and speaking.

Marriage became a marathon as long as your attention span.
The stillness of our lives—was it that you wanted to cut
like paper kites rip the sky's calm?

Water is always a surprise—hot or cold. And so a third
in a marriage—child or the shadow on the fence.
Both are outsiders.
Only one's shadow does not disappear with the sun.
The third, the third, the third is a bird whose smell
appears before it does. Perhaps like wrinkles before old age.

Once, things were not thrown. My parents' attic still has them—
spades without handles; rope, rubber band, ribbon, things that tie.
And broken taps: they might sprout water some day.
Their marriage was a present always wrapped for tomorrow.
Now there are only epigraphs. Yours, from Tagore:
'Pain...is what error is in our intellectual life.'
Mine, from the tailor.

You and I are now the third—a lifetime's strangers
without beaks feeding on an iterant holy betrayal.

Singular-Plural

You: Singular

Every wedding anniversary, we behave like mountaineers,
and pretend to have conquered distance.
The summit is still a misty metaphor.
You make purchases and call them 'presents'.
I recount obese details of a past that's lost its congruence.

Anniversaries are wall paint, a smoothening of pores.
They bring colour to the skin of a marriage,
and hide cracks where parasites evade mores.

By the eleventh, we are exhausted.
Imagination has become a fixed deposit.

Your presents arrive together:
binoculars for me, a telescope for you.
You ask me to watch birds during the day so that
you can watch the stars at night.

'Which is closer—the birds in your binoculars
or the stars in my telescope?' you ask.
'You,' I say, singular. And late laughter.
The whisper is a parody of the night the anniversary commemorates.
'Yes,' you say, your smile a new reincarnation,
'You *are* singular—from you begins my infinity'.

You: Plural

Until we were married,
I never bothered about the plural.
Singularity is better than singular,
you said the morning of our wedding.
The lineman disconnected the phone call.

All our troubles you blamed on a metaphor: age.
All our fights I blamed on the plural.
The birds in my binoculars settled in a cage.
We got our marriage certificate photocopied.
Your stars, middle-class to a fault, survive
on insurance policies. Our plural—
joint account, train compartments, trilogy—
gets thinner with each day.
The marriage becomes a metropolis—
you and I its anonymous citizens.

The singular buys a CCTV camera from eBay.

History

My memory keeps getting in the way of your history.
—Agha Shahid Ali

Dancing Girl, Mohenjodaro

There is her little Baluchi-style face with pouting lips and insolent look in the eye. She's about fifteen years old I should think, not more, but she stands there with bangles all the way up her arm and nothing else on. A girl perfectly, for the moment, perfectly confident of herself and the world. There's nothing like her, I think, in the world.

—Mortimer Wheeler, 1973

To imagine you dance is to cross the highway like a child
not knowing length from breadth. And then to ask the question—
Were you woman or child—with your hand on that waist?

History, like paedophilia, has a way of turning girls into women.
For man is like Time, impatient for chests to grow monuments.
5,000 years, fifty million textbook stares—of your hand on that waist.

For me in middle school, history curdling to hormone, *you* were
    Harappa.
You were the city's interior: Granary and the Great Bath.
Was that the male alphabet then—that hand on that waist?

Poets have had their muses—Neera, Laura, Matilde and Bonolata.
But I was only a student failing exams, and you history's dancing
    hall.
Dancer without feet, a patriot of dance—your hand on that waist.

That thinness of limbs, the geometry of bangles, and my teenage
    lust;
The trade and the travel, the marketplace in your shadow, the day's
    slap.
And nudity, a civilisation's top soil. Exams—and your hand on that
    waist.

'Pendulous lips': that phrase swam in me all night, fish and worm.
History, like desire, is all inside: you were its interior decorator besides.
Was that desperation or disobedience—your hand on that waist?

A dancer's statue is a cruel irony, motion in freeze. A lie, a siege.
Hair in a bun, audacious and fun, questioning John Marshall's
'Ha, young *aboriginal nautch girl?*'—with your hand on that waist.

You looked but didn't see—the museum hadn't wooed your eyes.
Harappa was a girl with three pendants on her neck. We eloped but could not escape history's racism—*his* hand on that waist.

Chemistry

I knew Chemistry would be worse, because I'd seen a big card of the ninety-odd elements hung up in the Chemistry lab, and all the perfectly good words like gold and silver and cobalt and aluminium were shortened to ugly abbreviations with different decimal numbers after them.

—Sylvia Plath

Elements in the Periodic Table

i.

Calcium

'7.7,' the blood report declares,
and I suddenly feel like a mother to my bones.
They, those lines and arcs, over which
flesh and skin are glued like a late promise—
my children are in need.
But my body is poor in its reserves.
From where is the calcium to come?
I ask doctors, consult the internet,
I behave like a teenager on a diet.
Every few minutes, I tap my bones
to check for the sound of a crack,
as if I was an oyster and the fracture a pearl.
At first my knee, then my wrist, finger on finger—
everywhere except my stomach, where there's no bone.
I think about the many glasses of childhood milk
that I've emptied into the kitchen sink's mouth.
Its whiteness is now a moral:
the basin legs must have more calcium than me.
Overnight my definition of poverty changes:
suddenly everyone is richer than me,
their bones more precious than all I have in the bank.
I become a living laboratory,
my routine a set of prohibitions: 'Don't...'.
I bend my knee in guilt like a repentant pariah;
I work on the computer, alert to the crime I commit on my spine;
I look at my fingernails and admire their sad beauty.
I forget myself in the middle of a lecture.
The reason is a sudden sting of envy:
the chalk in my hand, my tool and my prop,
has more calcium than I ever will.
If only I could eat it like the blackboard does.
'But you never had children?' a colleague consoles kindly,
turning my unborn into calcium-sucking Draculas.

On TV, Michelle Obama is hula-hooping,
there's her calcium-buttressed hips.
I change the channel. Suddenly all goes quiet.
Floods, rain, bones, corpses; the hills
are breaking into landslides in Uttarakhand,
there where the gods are bathed in milk.
And still the hills didn't have enough calcium?

ii.
Iron

I know that love makes us hypochondriacs.
But that its flag should run through
my body as liquid, a red road,
is always a surprise.
Iron, its deficiency, makes of me
a nation without border patrol.
So the easy invasion on my margins—
fingertips, underside of eyes, lips.
Pinch-press-pull-prick. Blood should rise
like a patriarch, out to defend.
Doctors scold, nurses become teachers.
But my scores never reach the pass mark.
8 or thereabouts—my highest score.
Anaemia could be the name
of a colourless flower.
Like zinnia or petunia.
I ingest things that bleed—
beetroot, pomegranate, liver.
And banana—fruit, flower, stem,
all that leave sticky scars on white.
Nothing helps. Nothing happens.
And so infiltration: blood in a bottle.
When I am discharged, foreign,
a stranger's blood-passport running
through me, a feminist friend comes to visit—
'Why is it always an "Iron Woman"
but a "Man of Steel"?'
Another joke on 'dependent visa' is born.

Biology

Did laboratory studies affect my poetry? I am sure they did. I found the biology courses—minor, major, and histology—exhilarating. I thought, in fact, of studying medicine. Precision, economy of statement, logic employed to ends that are disinterested, drawing and identifying, liberate—at least have some bearing on—the imagination, it seems to me.

—Marianne Moore

Illness in Instalments

i.
Hospital

Illness rinses my insides
while I wait for you
to dye my hair.
Syringes and needles
lie carcass to a past
in my blood.
You like colour.
My paint is dark sputum,
sunlight a walking stick
with which you reward me.
We repeat passwords
of bank accounts.
Sweet lime, pomegranate,
apple, banana:
you fill my canvas
with demons of promises.
My tongue drains of its mother.
You scold me
in unfamiliar languages.
I sit straight in bed,
my spine in ballet.
'Good Health' is a skit
I now rehearse every evening.
The doctor claps
with stethoscope beats.
He borrows the sound
of my heart
for his orchestra.
You plan, like an ant
who's suddenly discovered

this season's immortality.
You hold my hand
as if it were an umbrella
you are opening into the rain.
You plug my ears
with your fingers:
the world is a firecracker
whose sound
you're guarding me from.
But I can hear what they say.
I see it in their calendar faces.
You move wispy hair
from my forehead.
You count time in finger taps.
Convalescence arrives
like an unfulfilled expectation.
You treat health like bed linen,
ironing out its creases
around my body.
You teach me how to breathe,
to steal air from its march past.
You stir spoons in empty glasses,
you scold the thermometer,
you calculate, you wait
for my fever to dissolve
into inconsequential sweat.
You promise to take me home
as if I was a newly wed bride.
You talk of the past
as if it was the future.
And when my body begins
making my future a past,
you look at me
as if I was an old photograph.
I wait for a new album.

ii.
Tuberculosis

This disease makes of my life an untruth—
a long corridor of fasting.
Food and its epigrams of cure
accuse me of a career of neglect.
The rewards of weakness are few:
almost none, except a lover's tourist care.
Every morning I am measured against myself.
I watch my shadows shrink into parenthesis.
Everything gets smaller—the dent on my pillow,
my signature on letters; and life.
Only my dreams stretch like elastic.
That, and the day. At night I am Keats,
sometimes Kafka, even Lawrence,
staring at death's deep cleavage.
By day I'm a hospital poet.
But even my bones had strength once:
it carried the weight of your poems, you forget.

iii.
Ulcer

The world's mouthwash drains
into my gullet. The slap of acid
beat by beat, a fresco of corrosion
in the oesophagus. That beauty is
an untouchable the doctor spies on—
the betrayals of endoscopy.
All great art comes from suffering.
Now I know the pain of canvasses
as they are pinched by paint.
All sounds grow faint:
the crowd of pain is a roar
that drowns all other secrets.
I stay up to give it company.

I eavesdrop on hospital gossip
and watch the night fold into
an anthology of obituaries.

iv.
Surgery

More knives have cut through me than men.
Insurance agents avoid me: I'm a 'hospital whore'.
Needles no longer prick, they are an arsenal of nostalgia.
The chart in the nurse's hand is a history textbook
doctors consult for reference. Vials annotate.
'To' and 'OT' form a palindrome around
which anaesthesiologists embalm my heartbeat.
Womanhood is an ambulance
screaming red light from a moving vehicle.
White. Distant. Only one mark of red.
It bleeds to no one's command.
Nurses talk about ageing as if it were a disease.
But men were once like trees, valued for age rings.
Nothing changes, almost nothing, the doctors say,
only a gradual slowing of the movement of oars
on a river I thought I'd tamed forever.
When I return home, restored but never quite the same,
I discover that death is always a hobo.
Now, all the news is on the neighbour's TV,
all the aroma in yesterday's leftovers.
Only the first night home after surgery
is what the day once was:
a reservoir of movement, the uterus a fledgling
insect trapped in marmalade on toast.

v.
Stool

I force the previous day's history into a bottle—
my innards a newspaper, a daily bulletin.
It's the only true history book—a communal sewer.
When I hand it to the woman at the clinic,
she sticks a label and writes my name.
My by-line, the day's ingestation
of the violence in my gullet justifies itself.

In the afternoon, the DeskJet printer screeches into a taunt.
The country's a hospital.
My 'Stool Report'.
Breaking News: 'Parliament passes a new law'.

A new diet is born.

Touch

Touch was a poem you taught me
to read. 'Aaa'—you tore the sound
out of my throat. You traced it out
for me to repeat. You became carbon
paper. Strokes-scratches-scribbles. I'm
the desert, you said. Touch. Become
my dune. I was sand, shy at first. I got
into your eyes. You rubbed me
into your lids. We hurt, we bruised,
we grew sore-pink. My hazelnut screams
filled your mouth. 'Eee'. And teeth came
on skin. Touch.

Touch was a seven-storeyed building
I climbed that pollen-yellow afternoon. You
lay on your back. I was da Vinci. I drew you.
One wasn't enough. I needed more. Bookshelves
of fingers. I piled you on you. Vitruvian
Man of my touches. Chimney smoke sneaked
into the room. A neighbourhood of shadows
leaned against our bed. You stood
with your back to me. Empty,
like an owl at noon. You left your eyes
on the bed. You touched the bluegreen
shadows on the floor with your toe. I
grew jealous. I called out to you. I
became a fisherwoman. I threw
my net out to you. Touch
was your suicide. You jumped in. What
gravity. Pleasure was a canal
you ploughed a stream into. Soles brushed
soles, luscious veins squeezed
to bulbs of moist delight, sweat hummed

in folds. You peeled
my scars away. Touch.

Touch was a season that year. Curtains
of stains hung like Cezanne on your back.
The wind stabbed like your thumb
at my chin. Touch was a parrot song. Your
feather breath on my neck. Powdered
light on your hair. Touch was a rope
we pulled too hard. It snapped in the air.
We went looking for ends but got only glue.
Touch was ripe grain you fed the birds.
Touch was a morning-wet road
you wanted to cross. You held
my sleeve, I stroked your clouds.

Touch was striped rain on my back. You
let my skin soak till you found a song. Touch
was a paper lantern you hung
from a tree. There's fire in roots,
you whispered, doodles of breath
around my navel. I burned.
Touch was a hand rubbing turmeric
on satin aubergine skin. My earlobe pressed
like oilseeds between your fingertips.

Touch was the railway track-spine
with habit-stops. You ploughed down
while the red flag fluttered in the wind.
You took palanquin-years to return. I waited,
licked stamps, posted letters to myself.
You built bridges, tattooed roads with touches
in other places. Touch. Touch
became a blind mirror.

We lost touch.

I became an untouchable.

Natural Science

I follow locusts. I think they're loyal, but it's a story.
—Rebecca Gayle Howell

Rain

Rain is your birthmark,
your drool,
your hamartia.
You were a Stupa.
I lacked courage.
I stayed on the ship.
I stood on the deck
and watched your
peace. Peace—
striped, thick and thin,
mossy. For who had last
touched peace?
What peace there is
in falling!
Lazy peace.
Peace is obedience,
the ancient call
of gravity.

Rain,
I only see you grow,
unbidden,
into a silver music,
into a skeleton of ruins.
Rain,
I long
to touch your toes,
to pull them outwards,
to crackle them,
to let my cousins hear
how I make love
to your slippery body.

Rain,
I sew myself
on to river floors
sometimes
and wait like a secret
resting on her elbow.
Rain,
let me nurse
your calluses,
let me tease
out your blackheads,
let me,
let me
bear you a child,
an inheritor of your soft fins.
Rain,
cover my throbbing veins tonight,
tell me
that your ancestor
wasn't a pirate on a smudgy sky.
Rain,
tell me that I'm a thud
on your translucent skin.
Rain,
tell me that
I'm the lover
you lost last August,
that you've only come
to lick my blisters,
to collect the last word
I threw at you.
Rain,
tell me that you love
my shimmer of sins,
my pageant of pain,
that all I want scrubbed

from the throat of my life,
you want to hold in your blood,
that you want my insomniac sighs
to slip between your fingers.
Rain,
tell me that you will come
to the stone fair with your dog.

We will make fever.

Umbrella

Let me rinse
out the water
from the bones
of the earth.
They clog your
pregnant motion.

Look at the rain,
its elephantine gait,
its ivory mood.
Let me wait
for the rain
to stop its
parasitic fall
into your
umbrella's armpits.

This is a vase
in which you harvest
my flesh and your broom.
My umbrella has no memory.
The odour of time,
as it bleaches bones
of hope, sticks
like water droplets
to its taut spoke-ends.
Like you, they are adamant.
They defy gravity.

The umbrella is a rind
you prepare to peel
every sunny day.
I say it's an inverted
spittoon collecting the sky's

sadist sweat. You disagree.
Inside the umbrella
we share the clouds
unequally. We hide
limp and loss,
and nurse love
as if it were bee-stings.
You spin it around—
I see the spokes
mesh into a
nasturtium of sin.
I want to withdraw,
but the colour-blind rain
pleats you and me
into a chocolate slab.
I wait to crack,
the fissure between us—
babble, breasts and teeth.

The umbrella's a prison,
its loves a memory,
like milk teeth.
I am needy
in my longing
for amnesiac lungs
and knitted skin.

The umbrella closes
unto itself. All
turns middle.
Home. Wife. Crow.
You become
someone else's
prayer again.
And then,
the umbrella

prepares its skin
to let you fall,
together,
like paralysed strangers,
you and the rain.

Physics

*Start from nothing
and let the sound reach you.*
—Peter Gizzi

'Are You Lonesome Tonight?'

The door opens itself
into a cave: it holds
a lover's night.
A caged monsoon.
The room is its own
prisoner. It handcuffs
a silence to the bed.

The day waits
to grow complete.
How can it,
without you?
You are its pillow
at the end of a bed,
the day's backrest.

Socks become balls
in shoes, the shirt
droops for attention
on the old chair's
hard shoulders.
The hankie grows old
in my pocket. It misses
your nitpicking,
your stabs at its stains.
Every hotel-room night,
I want to escape with you
to a life without nights,
where days end,
not into the darkness
of electric switches,
but into you,

where I'm stitched,
as holy books to ears,
into the leather
of your dreams.

Biraha

Love makes of everyone
a parent. All distances
seem too long, all moments
a first-aid kit on call.
Time becomes a zoo—
our past a caged animal.
Love is an accent
that needs practice.
Where are you?
This—this life's grass,
the unread books,
secret tickets,
moon and brass—
needs a room
with shadows.
Come. Come home.

This distance isn't safe anymore.

I feel bereft,
I watch my nails grow,
I become my own prison.
How do you sleep
without your pillow?
I see myself turn
into a weekend,
into ellipses,
into your likeness.
You are my paperweight,
holding me back from air.
Once you tampered
with my restraint,
put my goodbyes in orbit.
Now I'm at war with aloneness,

like the lost shoe of a pair.
Without you, I am nothing.
I'm a winter month,
hawking darkness at the fair.

These letters I write to you,
these dolls of trance,
turn you into new ghosts,
our love into a séance.
Why this absence,
these cruel vowels
that keep you away?
This love, this need for friction—
skin and bristles, teeth's tentacles—
is superstition? This is death
if there is death at all.
These tears, these long solstices,
are all love's pension.
And you'll still say that biraha
is only the fourth dimension?

Long-distance Relationship

Every relationship is a long-distance relationship:

Every poem a letter
Every prayer a curiosity

Every goodbye a question
Every return a going-away

Every longing a sigh
Every embrace a withdrawal

Every tiff an awakening
Every patch-up a hibernation

Every whisper an alarm clock
Every sneeze a calling bell

Every touch a telegram
Every tickle a missed call

Every relationship is a long-distance relationship

Geography

Licence my roving hands, and let them go
Before, behind, between, above, below.
O, my America, my Newfoundland,
My kingdom, safest when with one man mann'd
—John Donne

Nicosia

i.
Arrival
Mediterranean.

Me di ter ra ne an.
Even dreams can be polysyllabic.
(This one as old as the Orient Longman schoolbook.)

When you first see it from above
you think of all its relatives that you've met before—
the sea in Bombay and Puri, the bays, even ponds—
but nothing prepares you for your dream lover; or for this.
No relatives, no superstitions, no dreams.

Could this be the Mediterra...?
Its skin crinkled like it hasn't met oil ever.
Or been touched, its pores moisturised by a lover.

I am that lover it's been waiting for.
My curiosity is stronger than light's.

The plane lands like a gimmick
as if it's about to land on water.
Like your image in the mirror.
Soundless and inevitable,
but still always a surprise.

The rest soon follow:
the eyes of my co-passengers—blue,
borrowed from the Mediterranean;
the sense of humour of immigration officers;
your thoughts and my thoughts of you,
background music coalescing with questions;
the Greek alphabet, as foreign and familiar as acidic spit.
Like your lover, they are a function of memory and invention.
And loss.

Then the elements.
A lone windmill, out of place.
Like a wrong punctuation.
All punctuation is inappropriate.
Everything except your expectation.

The sea is outside.
Everywhere.
Like you are inside me.
The sea is blood.
You're blue or red,
depending on where you are—
inside or outside me.

There are no houses here.
My eyes know this—
this landscape where you are the landscape
and also its intrusions.
These gentle mounds they call hills to amuse themselves,
like your body in liquid sleep.
The dwarfish conifers are a surprise
like a scar or raised boil on your skin.

The sea is now to my right.
Like you, lying next to me.
Both of you move gently in your sleep.
I'm always awake.
Like sand is to even a tiptoe.

Greek begins to sound like Tibetan.
The sound of the semi-foreign is perhaps always the same.
It's like the wind—
you know its behaviour though not its accent always.
The person you love is not here.
No lover is, in a moment such as this.

The air has the assurance of your breath on my shoulder.
When you lie on me, exhausted, collecting desire for a quick future.
All knowledge is second-hand.
Except this. This familiarity of breath, of home.
The only original.
You are that home. I breathe—that is my rent.

We, who share everything, like smokers do a fire,
knowing it to be generic but also private, like a secret,
know this—
that there's no 'local fish', no 'local guardian',
and no 'local poem'.

ii.
Departure

'People have been living here for 4,500 years.'
It's the manager of the hotel.
It's not the hotel he means (for my eyes have revealed their yolk)
but Nicosia, this leaf-shaped city,
curling at the edges, as if life were permanently autumn.
A leaf floating on water.

Standing on the hotel verandah,
its iron grille shaped like a shy smile
(so graceful, it could only have been a leftover from sleep),
I think of you and our love—
whether it's older than death,
and whether this city is older than death.
There are verandahs everywhere
(like pockets in buildings),
as if life was meant only for looking
and waiting, to weigh the breeze,
to feel longing for what is beyond one's reach,
or to treat the sky as an uninhabitable island.
To stand on them is to be an amphibian,
living both inside and outside.

Stephanos Stephanides is here.
He's this island's poet—
it's in the name already,
like Euripides,
monyms that carried Greece across water.

I know this day of May will be the day
The dead will awaken only once
Next spring will be too late...
Even the dead do not wait forever
I've met his words before I meet him,
his hand on his beard,
pulling hair when in thought,
as if thinking was a stringed instrument.
I do not know why I think of Plato or Socrates,
the lonely intelligence of bearded Greek men.

There's a Green Line that divides Nicosia—
since only space can be divided, and not time,
the Greek Cypriots claim the South,
the Turkish Cypriots the North.
We do not go North—
there are warnings, of blood in its wind,
as if violence is any less where we are,
at home, or in the heart.
But we listen—
obedience is a virtue in foreigners.
That marks a tourist from a soldier.

In the Walled City—
past Ledra Street (The Murder Mile)
where beauty spills from tiny shops
on to narrow streets like buck teeth,
and Faneromeni Square,
where the beauty of the churches convinces you
that ancient man imagined god as an aesthete—
is a restaurant that is about to close.

Stephanos speaks softly,
in a language that is tentative,
as if it's just about to come to fruition.
Here one eats what the family cooks for lunch.
Vegetables from the island fill our tiny table
like a train whistle filling the mind of a village.

Wrapped like a gift is the Cypriot dolma—
vine leaves hugging meat and rice
like bark does cambium.
It opens twice—
first barely on my plate,
then inside my mouth,
meat and rice resting against each other,
like sleep on pillow.
The memory of paturi—
fish wrapped in banana leaf,
the genius of fire in its taste—
builds new walls inside my mouth.

My mind, like a fly in summer,
moves to you, again—
every moment's a letter despatched to you.
Now, behind me, is the Byzantine museum,
and then the Kykkos monastery,
its lines as strong as suspicion.

Standing at the Freedom Square,
that connects the old city to the new,
like only a photo album can,
I think of our love, its brown streets,
and you, my 'local poem'.

Death by Darjeeling

You are grateful that the wind doesn't cast shadows.
When you spot it testing the arrogance of flowers,
you reach out to protect their torn shadows.
You are already Darjeeling's prisoner:
you mistrust your watch—
how can its hands hold the death of daylight?

Because rain is always a trespasser, you carry the fear like a secret:
wetness is always a surprise, its body an earthworm.
There is Giri Niwas and Sharma Cottage and Lama Building,
but before all of these is Madhu-di's shop,
her voice like a sleepy pigeon,
asking why you've stopped buying tomatoes.
You say something about the colour red.
'They killed Madan Tamang near the Planter's Club...'
Age has done her life great violence—
now only her shop can hold her girth.
Her words move at the speed of hunger:
'Death digests everyone in Darjeeling.'

On Lebong Cart Road are the town's children.
There is always a newborn on someone's lap.
Here the streets are nurseries.
Children are born. Crematoriums grow.
Even the dead must be employed—
so they bring in tourists.
Pilgrims hunting for ancestry in damp soil,
that makes life look like an immigrant. Death is a drug.
Candles, flowers without baptisms, silk khaada.
You see your breath turning to cold smoke
and you wonder why the dead should only be respected.

Later you apologise to yourself, for this wayward meanness—
it is only the wickedness of sorrow, this long tourism of illness,
the failure to remember that you were also dead once.
To your right is Happy Valley, where tea is more expensive than gold.
On the left lies the Hungarian linguist Alexander Koros.
Both need strangers and the secret education of tongues—
the man, his picket fenced language; and tea.
You hear the accent of its history in the crack of the blue china.
And you think of death as a season—why else would it return?

You begin to concede that there is only one season in Darjeeling:
it lives inside throats of hawkers at Chowrasta—'tourist season'.
Here, at the town centre, severed heads of men were hung once:
traitors, they thought Gorkhaland was cartilage. Violent hermits.

The clouds nudging the hills are blotting paper.
They will wipe away these blisters of sight.
All the tourists need is the mountain sun.
A metaphor to trap a holiday.
And so Tiger Hill, its sunrise and sunset a Darjeeling day held in
    parenthesis.

In your sleep you hear the tourists move, walk on socks and shiver,
you hear the jealousy of rain and their search for the sun,
the holiday's beauty spot. Your dreams search for a corridor,
the sun for a camera, its right to love outsiders.

In your stolen sleep, two things are turning into statues—
a tree and its dying shadow; the other is a poet with a placard.
On the placard is the horoscope of a poem,
its words gathering into a murmur, collected futures,
words its caged warriors: 'Gorkhaland, Gorkhaland.'

Revolutions, like dreams, begin untitled.

Finding Light in Sukna

The winter morning rises—
an old cough, sputum that tucks
itself in crevices of the iris.
A white crane carries
the sunlight in its beak and
dissolves it into the stream.
Light floats and fights, it
tires, and then, like an insect,
sucks out the day all at once.
Light is honey. It sweetens the
sight. And then it disappears.
Light is honey.

Light is a schoolboy walking
on a river, a prophet with a
stick. Light is a command.
Light is an untouchable girl
playing hopscotch on the
river. I wait, I play, I throw
a stone in the Sukna. A black
stone, blacker in the river, fights
with light. It loses. Light takes its
revenge—the stone turns
twig, long is round, and all
straight crooked. Light on the
Sukna.

Light is a promise
you said you'd keep. You'd
bring light and take some—from
Sukna.

You sneezed first,
and it shook. Light on the
Sukna.

Light is a
child you throw to the sky. Gather,
collect, hold. Light is a cracked heel
on the Sukna. Nurse.
You were a lover,
you thought light was the sound of
an animal you wanted to capture,
to shoot, and tame. You threw out
a lasso to the light on the Sukna.
Like a lover
you returned—burnt. A singed
film roll—of light on the Sukna.

Night by the Torsha

Night's your nickname,
you swore by the Torsha—
and the cow-heel black night
became me.

Night is a scratch,
a blue-black bruise going sore,
you cursed, dipping the ends
of my hair in the Torsha. The
wet dripping joy became the night.

Night is a neighbourhood
aunt you once eavesdropped
on. She's going blind. Her breasts
sag, you say. They feed the day.

Night is excess bleeding
the sky. Night is light, light
looking at itself. Night is light
cleaning itself. Night is light
scrubbing your eyes.

You
watch but cannot see.
Look, there's the night
seeping into the breath
of trees. Hear, there's
the night licking the roof.
Hear, hear, the night's
lapping. Shadows undress.
Night, night. Night is a refrain
without repetition. Night is pure.
Night. Night is a thief never
caught stealing. Night, night.
Night is a clothesline
sniffing at the wind. Night.

Torsha tickles the night.
The river's a mat on which
the night rubs its feet. You
held my feet in your palms.
Soft. Tighten, you said,
commanding the night.
The skin creased. Stars
burst into shivers, the
night was a hiccup in
the Torsha.

Night is a discipline, the
Torsha taught us. We ran
errands for it. You blew
my hair away from her face,
I helped her swallow
your tickles. And our skin,
our sticky unknowingness,
soaked the mint night.
Night.
Torsha swallowed
the night. You held it on
your tongue. And then
you poured the basil leaf
night down my throat.
And the night was cured.

Home Science

The houses are haunted
By white night-gowns.
—Wallace Stevens

House

My love,
my love, is my forehead
on which you scatter grains
for pigeons every morning.
My smile is a courtyard,
my reclining shadow a cowshed,
my scalp the moon-skin's song,
my throat an old mossy well,
my hands a windmill that crush scented air,
my ears the mauve flower
that begins to hear with the day,
my legs, my legs a canal
that bring the flow of anklets your way,
my mouth a betel leaf you fold and chew for taste,
my eyes a post box you steal letters from,
and my eyebrows—my eyebrows
a ladder you climb to pluck sleep.

I was your house without a roof.

The birds saw me
shaping my nails every evening.
They dropped thin moons
on my lake-like nails.
You called them woks
and fried my smiles in them.
They smelled good—the smiles,
as they shrivelled
in scalding oil.
I wanted to smile
but was scared to show you
the one spare smile
I'd saved in the cow's udder.

My nails were flags that I put out
to flutter and scratch the wind.
My bindi was a cowdung cake
slapped against your back.
I dried in the sun,
your finger marks stabbed and wrinkled
and grew old with me.

Sunlight was superstition.
I'd wither and weather
if you touched me
in the light, you said.
So darkness.
Its grassy smell,
its guilty moistness,
its uncertain sagging skin,
its tropical climate,
its humid love,
its sticky inconsequentiality.

Darkness.
You hid me in it,
like a dog does his bone.

My body became your family.
My shadow, changing
to the mood of your tongue,
your mohalla.
You spat betel-leaf juice on my walls.
I bled.
And as the evening wringed the sky of light,
darkness seeped into my hinges.
Doors and windows.
Mouth and burrow.
You lit a kerosene lamp at my feet.
Fire grew to smoke,
water bubbled to a murmur,

tapped my lid,
I burst open.
The wick burned all night.
It sucked oil,
it smoked,
it smudged new glass.
It grew thin.
I was a log of wood.
I was kitchen.
I was clay oven.
I was coal.
I was roti—
dough pressed between your fingers
and flattened to smoothness.
I was roti,
breakfast and dinner,
I was roti,
swelling up with heat,
I was roti,
caught between your teeth.

I was so many other things besides:
Cup and plate, jug and glass, lock and key,
all pairs that hold a house in embrace.

My clay body,
drying with the wind,
melting in the rain;
you plastered clay on clay,
every day,
until only outside was my all,
and my inside was only a bamboo,
an axis around which men
left behind tattoos of their slaps.
All men are, in the end, only masons.

There were cowries on my skin,
half-slit open. One-eyed cowries
as if in a permanent wink.
I was a pagoda of fireflies,
I glowed in the light.
No one noticed me burn.

I was perfect, you said.
Only I had no hair on my head.

Yet you brought flowers for me
to wear in my hair.
For flowers made your dream woman—
a farmer's wife.
Yellow mustard flowers,
sharp to the nose, ambitious,
a future granary;
Sthalapadma, lotuses of the land,
lotuses without sharp spouts;
You climbed trees for me,
from there you told me stories of the sea.
You saw what I couldn't see—
you saw water, I saw distance.
For space was an alphabet
you hadn't cared to learn.
You hung marigolds from walls.
I didn't care for ceilings.
You didn't want height.
Hair was false height, you said.
You were looking for depth.
You dug for wells.
You dug for ponds.
You wanted fish.
You wanted rod.

I was only a house.
How could I move?
I waited, I watched.

You held it like a curse.
You held it like a rope.
You held it like water.
You held it like hope.

The nose! The nose?
And the nose is all you missed?
You said you were looking for oars,
for sail, for mast, for air;
The nose is a ship?

The nose ring's only a loop
that brings the cows home.
We had none, not cows,
not fragments of footprints
to sew on to our new history.
Why ships then? Why homecoming?
Why the quiet doodles of nose rings?
Why bird-bites on wood-carvings?
Why half-circles of summer foam?

Nose ring was a world with a pinch,
you said; it was the world's boundary.
Life's frame—round with a leak,
allowing death a peek.
You treated it, at first, like a fishing hook,
You wanted me to bite,
Then you wanted it to bite me.

You thought it was a waistband
you'd tie around your world,
You thought it was a snake
that would bite its own tail.

I was only a house.

You punctured my earlobes with it.
Buttermilk accusations ran like pus.

You gathered folds of skin with it.
The nose ring became pincers.
You sewed my blouse ends with it.
The nose ring became a door latch.
You pushed our fingers inside it.
The nose ring became our love's wallet.

It became all you wanted it to be.
But you wanted more.

You were a man.
I was only a house.

And so you brought stone,
You brought hammer,
You'd tired of roundness, you said.
You hit it hard, you hit it strong,
The circle fumbled, then crawled,
It wanted its shape back.
You hit it hard again.
It became snail,
It became earthworm,
And then a matchstick that wouldn't light.

Even anthill bricks are round,
You sometimes say,
And earrings and bangles,
And necklace and rings,
Only roundness suits a woman,
Men wouldn't have it any other way.

The world is a woman, and so is the moon,
The plough is a woman, and so are stories.
You rolled the nose ring on my skin,
It became wheels and crushed me.
It became a ball at your feet.
You were a man,
Your feet found joy in roundness.

And I still wanted you.
What good is a house without snores?

All you wanted was my left,
My room and a wall—
The nose ring was a clothesline
You wanted to hang babies from.
But you loved its purdah the best:
Such neat divisions, you said,
A mucus-dark andar mahal,
locked from inside with a half-bitten key;
the man's world, like land,
hanging, sloth-like, for all to see...

A nose ring was a mirror
that held the future of faith,
A nose ring was a summer day,
only a winter comforting thought.
You said such things and pierced my skin,
A nail on my wall, a crumbling chandelier within...

You are a man.
I'm only a house.

'Good Housekeeping'

At night, after you close the day like a book,
you grope for a bookmark.
That is peace, the house's morphine,
for which you pay the bank interest.
The neighbour switches off the lights—
darkness becomes a sound.
The moonlight rests somewhere on the terrace,
making of your house its inn.

On a day like today,
you want to send your house on a holiday,
knowing that it will return to you
like a little child does, when thrown up into the sky.
Once the house was your child.
Now you are its slave.
It behaves like a pensioner.

(There are the cobwebs, the house's cuticles,
always in need of paring.
Dreams make the skull of a house, you know.
You spend your life looking for the house's tail.)

Once, camels could pass through eyes of needles.
I laughed at the folly of my ancestors.
Now, as if in revenge, the three-storeyed house passes through my
    eyes.
I see other things—impossibilities:
It is possible to hate humans, even those we love,
but your house?
Love returns after every bout of housekeeping,
like saliva in your mouth.

So every night you lock the gate.
And the boundary wall becomes an engagement ring.

Chair

And you still sit on it,
sometimes,
in my moon-dust mind.
Your toes touch the floor
like a crane's old beak,
searching for the certainty
of slipperiness.
Your slippers rest,
like an ant's winter
on the amnesiac floor,
the ancient promise
of gravity.
Your hands are a mask—
I inspect for tear on the rest.

I envy the chair
its shy contentedness,
its archive of postures,
its vessel of lightness,
its handkerchief lap.
I envy the chair
its easy godness—
the way it holds you
without a lover's purpose
or bitter vanity.

It's a statue about loss—
You sat here.

A pound of shadow
perspires in my memory.
I search for it,
for veins of olive-skinned
desire that once was yours.

I put my nails
into secret chambers
of March-dried bubbles
of poison.
I dig for some sign
that would bring you,
once, just once,
to life, to my lamppost-life.

Death is cruel,
memory is crueller,
love's nudity cruellest.
I search for my marriage
in this chair,
in its banyan-tree edges,
as if it were a photo-frame
that held a sense of you,
a casteless sense.
The chair's a calendar
of sitting events:
its teakwood enthusiasm,
its clotheshorse detachment
its umbrella self-centredness...
carry you farther away from me.

How could you leave?
For the strange,
for sexless death?
This I find most hateful—
that you loved me,
but loved me less,
loved death more.

Sitting on a chair
is circumcision.
A secret disease that is
its own cure.

Like my bone of love—
its own province.

'Losing a woman is punya,
Losing a river is sin…'
you said, sitting here.
And losing a man?
All that's left now
is a wayward disease—
one you plucked
from a woman's oven
and gave me.
Dying is an art
you taught me
on this chair.
Now there's only
the colour of sleep,
the invention of names
and this chair,
a lyric pyre.

General Knowledge

I have no reserve knowledge, no provisional knowledge. And everything that I learn, I learn for a particular task, and once it's done, I immediately forget it, so that if ten years later, I have to get involved with something close to or directly within the same subject, I would have to start again from zero, with some few exceptions.

—Gilles Deleuze

Sunlight

You trapped sunlight like a tree.
Every autumn you wanted to take a new lover—
pet, clothes, toy.
You thought adulthood a disease.
Your torn shoes made our lives a museum of journeys.

I remind myself that you were only nine.
I remind myself that you'd asked me Ma Kali's age
and how you always said you were older than her.

In Vrindavan, you said you wanted to be a widow.
You liked white. Its taste, you said, was what
you wanted to be: a tube of toothpaste in our mouths.

When your brother threw up in the car,
you cupped your palms.
Vomit was precious, you said.
One day you'd be vomit too, you promised.

Your catalogue of ambitions grew like nails.
You counted backwards to your birthday every morning,
restless to be ten.
'I'll change my name to "Decade",' you said.
"Decade" is prettier than "Dopati", your name, you argued.

Your grandmother had named you after the flower,
but you wanted to be Time, not sweet-smelling.
Time has more chlorophyll than all the trees in the world.

When they brought you to us that Friday morning,
blood sticking to your legs like a creeper,
your brother pointed to the sunlight lake inside your frock.
Tomorrow I'll be the sun, you'd told him, planning for fancy-dress
    fun.

There were bottles inside you, and male snot.
A syringe in your hair. A button in your palm.

I do not remember the rest. Your father still seals our broken window panes with posters of 'Save the Girl Child'.
Your grandmother stares at sunshine's death certificate.

(A five-year-old girl was raped in Delhi in the summer of 2013—a candle and a 200 ml bottle of hair oil were found inside her.)

'Every Girl Is Dinner'

(From Swati Moitra's photograph of Vishwavidyalaya Metro Station at North Campus, Delhi University)

I passed through daughterhood
like a young goat crossing a highway
one wrong step and I could be dead.
(Men, Baba said, were automobiles,
lust an accident, my body rush-hour traffic.)

Before school hour, I sat like a sparrow
on a cow horn—destiny's bisexual perch,
waiting for a companion
with whom I could take flight.
For that is the moral of sparrow life:
One for sorrow, Two for joy,
Three for letter, Four for boy.
('Walk in groups, always';
'Aekla chalo re is for men alone'.)

Sometimes I am chicken—
my legs, swollen from captivity, a delicacy.
I am a kilometre virgin,
never having tested the speed of my soul.
In neighbour's curries, my feet cast no shadow.
I am a 'good girl', 'nutritious' when stewed.

All my life, I've always been meat—
goat, sparrow, poultry;
my tongue eaten raw, like a bull's;
my fingers giving a vegetable its name;
my body chopped into pieces for temple retail—
Puri, Kamamkhya, franchises of barbecue religion.
Ma Shakti: 'Shakti Peeth' to 'Shakti Mills'.

I hear the phrases tune their strings
in the fibrous appetite between teeth,
in the butcher's bleeding blades.
The alliterations in a pair: rape and rage,
cannibal lust, carnivorous anger,
words, the world as slaughter house,
violence as scansion, violation as eating.
Woman as kebab, woman in a tandoor.

And I wait, a living carcass,
my life bullied into cold storage,
to surrender my meathood.

Philosophy

The family is one of nature's masterpieces.
—George Santayana

Marriage in Hostage

Marriage is paper folded into two.
It looked the same from both sides
once. Now an outside waits
on an inside. Glass is settlement.

Marriage is rheum, the eye's plea
for justice. Fairness its leftover.
The child is a snout they mistake
for a carom pocket. Adultery is Scrabble.

Marriage was a gait they wore without
mirrors. Bed sheet creases were doodles
they hid from the maid. Love was bling,
the pigeon's doob doob. Night is a lisp.

Marriage is a metal that swallows
fingers. It clanks like a vulture's gizzard.
Hostages busk of wheat and whistles. Silence
twitches like a nerve. Talk is a G-minor drone.

Silent Night, Holy Night

If you are afraid of loneliness, do not marry.
—Anton Chekhov

Once, I was the artist in our marriage,
now my unfinished masterpiece.
You sharpen scalpels, I craft my nightmares.
I walk down never-ending stairs.

Silent night, holy night,
All is calm, all is bright

Every night now, we pretend to forget—
the season of miscarriages, the awkwardness
of over-familiarity, the smell of socks
hardening into leftovers.
We fold mistakes like clothes,
keeping them alive for another day.
Errors turn into kettle-fossils.

Sleep in heavenly peace,
Sleep in heavenly peace

'Not today…'

Your sleep is our marriage's dowry.
Watching you sleep, I feel like a car
being overtaken by another.
Only there's no speed—
your breath paces slower than mine.
I watch this ticketless travel carry you away.
I worry about the long queue that makes me
wait to get into your dreams.

Silent night, holy night

Half-asleep, the ancient tremulousness
of hunting sticking to eyelids,
we scratch with words, blunt weapons.
We win sigh-battles.
God is a pillow we fight with.
Role-playing master, he becomes arbiter.

Silent night, holy night,
Shepherds quake at the sight

A wife is never porn, I say.
Is it the same for dreams? I ask.
Your sleep's tarmac keeps me away.

But it wasn't always like this.

I wish we were old. Or older.
Young jasmine bulbs have no fragrance.
Youth must have had its uses—

Glories stream from heaven afar,
Heavenly hosts sing Alleluia!

Our marriage was young once.
We slept better, we forgave more,
we excreted more rheum.
Problems were a frame
that gave our lives structure,
like a wallet does to currency notes.

Middle-age is the season of plenty:
more food in the trash than in stomachs,
clothes for six lifetimes, the seventh ajar.

Radiant beams from Thy holy face
With the dawn of redeeming grace

Now I sit with the cherry seed in my mouth,
caught between swallowing and spitting,
trapped in the cubicle between abundance
and being abandoned.

Silent night, holy night

Secrets

> *I want to be with those who know secret things or else alone.*
> —Rainer Maria Rilke

You often tell me that you know all my secrets—
my lust drawn in forest ink,
the way I find beauty monotonous,
my ketchup art of kisses.

I disagree.

We've shared a canopy of love signs for too long.
We've been bandaged together for comfort.

Youth, I see now, was a ticketless curse.
Do you remember how we found each other there—
spit-fresh after our violently normal childhoods?
For years I wiped secrets off your shadow,
until my skin and rag became one.
The soluble intimacy of sandalwood and water
is an invitation to lethargy in a marriage.

We'd lost what had once been most precious:
secrets, them in clusters.
By oath, we've become each other's keeper
of secrets and bones.
In doing that, we've lost ours.

Familiarity is a piggybank.
We drop coins, delight at its tingling, and forget.
There is no waiting, no holding back, no reserve.
Shyness is an EMI we have long paid off.
Now there are other interests.

And thereafter only the frenetic accumulation
of secrets, of secrets hardening into faults.

Education

I am not a teacher but an awakener.

—Robert Frost

Shanti: Niketans

i.

They cannot scare me with their empty spaces.
And so Frost walks beside me on red soil.
'Desert Places'. This too was a desert once.
The Tagore quote levitates inside my head:
'...dreary desert sand of dead habit'.
Bhuban-danga, the bank of the world—
This was all there was,
an inert land that Maharshi, the Poet's father,
transformed into a revolutionary,
bit by bit, massaging foreign soil on the red earth.
for even soil must be married for eugenics.
And so the gossip of green over my head—
trees from abroad, ferried home like trophies,
now gone native. Like the white woman in batik.

This emptiness
—this 'far from the madding crowd' hashtag—
has an erotics that only schoolteachers recognise.
For nothing speaks of lack of reciprocity
more than vacant school benches.
I recognise a teacher when I see one here:
their faces are like a call list filled with missed calls.
In this Shantiniketan, someone is always absent,
someone as necessary as instinct,
a memory without gender.
And so every tourist turns into a schoolchild.
For only here, education has still not become an antibiotic.

The tourists, their water-scratched plastic bottles,
their sandals embalmed with dust and disgust,
look for trash bins, garbage dumping sites,

as if they have come to bury
the genitalia of metropolitan life,
like students hide report cards.
It is terrifying, their urgent need to lose bathwater,
to become something only imagined backwards,
as if Shantiniketan were a sex-change surgery.
For what else is the man-at-peace except
the first line of an aborted story?

In their shrill touristy look-at-that voices,
I hear the whirr of ceiling fans.
And I suddenly discover,
when something gets into my eye,
that wind, like shanti, is a loanword.

ii.

Here,
in Shantiniketan (House of Peace),
a polysyllable that's survived
many gap-toothed accidents,
even god must be a tourist.
Or a rickshaw-puller.
Both looking for bargains.

I am suddenly aware of the relation
between sunlight and time.
In that I become a bird.
Amra Kunjo, the home amidst the mango trees.

Not thesaurus-sweetness attaching to mango seeds,
but leaves, their dark sex lives still unknown to man.
An orchard of quiet, solemn at first, then stainless,
like the back of a head in a concert hall.

Here Robi's father would meditate,
lose weight from his soul,
like sunlight on water,
I think I hear a tourist guide say.

Is it the water, the light, what,
that turns plebeians into poets here?
I ask aloud.
'This soil has a soul too.'
It's a young boy in khaki shorts,
a pair of binoculars hanging from his neck.
I smile. There is little else to give children these days.

But soon we are back to the bureaucracy of tourist life—
photo-taking, lost slippers, everyday myths.
Tagore-was-here; Tagore-did-this; This-tree-was-planted-by...
Sapling quotes, earthenware anecdotes, all fired for effect.
I am bored. I look at the boy. He adjusts his skull cap.
He is drawing a bearded man in his drawing book.
I wait for the lines to congeal, to become Tagore.
'Who is that?' I ask, like one can only ask children.
The little boy doesn't answer. Instead he scribbles.
My myopic eyes can only read the long-tailed T.
'Ah, that's Tagore,' I say, playing adult.
He shakes his head, no it isn't.
And then, like a grandchild,
he carries the notebook to my nose.
Below the Tagore-like sketch stands a lonely word:
'Terrorist'.
The boy has left his sign too: 'Tourist'.
Red ants drag me back to my feet.
We are all scratching, dragging nail-lines up to our thighs.
The bearded man watches over this democracy of pain.
The little boy folds the portrait into a paper cone—
his mother fills it with moori.
And Shantini turns into a world without daily bread.

iii.

On my way to Ratan Kuthi, 'guest house',
I grope for the day of the week.
In the sky is the stalker moon without a return address.
We've just had a fight about the length of holidays.
I've folded my wanderlust into an aphorism:
A holiday should be as long as the time between two haircuts.
He, editor on the prowl, tweaks 'haircuts' to 'two shaves'.

The metaphor's got into my eyes.
I don't see a single barber shop in Shantini.
(Is that why Tagore wore his hair long? I want to ask him.
But there's the tug-of-war silence epiloguing our tiff.)
Shanti, Shanti: my mother's dove-words float away.
This evening peace, this lie, is an amulet for marital warfare.
Darkness is collecting the day;
where's the janitor who collects quarrels?

In the distance is a familiar sound—
Is it a train? The TV? Streetcry?
Pressure cooker whistles sound the same everywhere.

We fall asleep without will, our heads on thin pillows,
sleep stapling us to the bed with Newton's gravity.
He mumbles something. I hear and do not hear,
as if it were a prophecy about our past.
'Did Tagore like his eggs sunny side up?'
I turn to my right, my legs around that question
as if it were a side pillow.
Sleep unites us at last, after the day's bargaining.
He sneezes. I think it sarcasm. He mumbles,
'Objectivity is a joke with one-sided laughter.'
An ambulance siren screeches through my sleep
all night. He claps when I wake up.
'You sleep like a woman in a painting
who shall never know an alarm clock.'

I sit up, out of breath,
the asphyxiation of unreturned calls.
'How would it feel to receive a missed call from Tagore?'

iv.

You do not notice dirt till it has dried, gathered
and collected itself into a memorial.
Shantiniketan is a conglomerate of dust.
Shanti: Must peace come only in dust?
Niketan. Home. House. And the dusty roads in between.
To say that this alone is the home of peace
is to deny its existence outside it.
Like a well does to dryness outside its circumference.
Or a foot outside a slipper.

Aachoo. Aachho.
This dust makes of me a minority,
reminds me of my living status.
And a future without holidays.
Here I notice dust in its green room,
as if it were a protagonist in an one-act play.
Dust and its asanas, an acrobatics of faith.

Suddenly Santiniketan turns into an extant manuscript.
For where else is dust such a well-fed resident?
In the archive in Rabindra Bhavan,
we take off our shoes and sandals.
And become employees of dust as researchers must.
All this until the sweeper's little son shouts to his father—
'Baba, I think Robi Thakur's statue is about to sneeze'.

The world—this Shantiniketan—turns into a dustbin.

v.

Here peace is a nocturnal habit.
Like an evening drink.
Its swollen feet rest outside
on the pebbled path,
fighting childhood science.

In Shantini, sunlight is food
inside stomachs and on canvasses.
What my eyes see is not life in a mosquito net,
trapped for an artist.

I will never see Tagore.
But his men are everywhere:
Nandalal, Binodbehari, Satyajit Ray, those whose nails he filed.
This place is now only a picture,
a tattoo of what might have been,
a motion picture, your eyes in your hands.
That, just for control. For your hands are traffic police.
Eyes, now put them in your wallet.

Outside Kala Bhavan, we rehearse the standing joke
that kills relationships and builds careers:
'Well begun is half done'.
An artist puts up his easel. A tourist poses.
Conscience is only hand-me-down elitism.
The painter puts a flower in the woman's hair.
In your love story you are always a maverick.
The world is marginalia, a loveless republic.

But she had come to be changed,
to be reassured that she wasn't
cellulose or iron, not yet.
She wanted to be the tympanum in his ear,
vibrating to every sound.
Instead she is now sifting through a godown of sounds.
She notices the traffic of curiosity behind sunglasses,

she listens to their eyes changing prepositions.
From the palette, where she is being formed,
she watches feet behave like fuel,
and cart forward precious ignorance.

Then she walks out of the canvas,
out into this small world, navigated on bicycles.
The painting is turning her blind.
She cannot see, she cannot see
inside the rickshaw-puller's mind
is the missing Malaysian aircraft.
When she bargains for the fare,
that secret tumbles out.
'Vanish,' he says, with magician-eyes.

You curse the sky for its monopoly of violence.
You become the girl in a painting, her eyes missing,
and you realise that your life is a folk tale without a moral.

Moral Science

We are all of us born in moral stupidity, taking the world as an udder to feed our supreme selves.

—George Eliot

Adult

You become an adult when you discover—

that shoes also cast shadows though we might stamp on them;
that a calling bell is not meant to alert but to prevent entries;
that even water can be impatient and sunlight a thing of tenancy;
that you actually slap yourself and not the mosquito.

You become an adult when you discover—

that you have become the subject of gossip;
that old love is centrifugal, new love centripetal;
that the human mind is a piece of furniture, and that dust settles
    on both;
that there is nothing that is more private than sleep;
and not that those we love will die, but that they must die.

But you actually become an adult when you first commit adultery.

Lust

The window's a quilt
I scratch with toes
in my finger-sleep.
Two men climb a coconut tree.
Their feet are tied with rope.
Coconut coir anklets scratch
their heels, pinch old bark.
They are a collage of waves
in my language-fever.
One climbs, the other slides—
gnashes of curiosity
on my amulet mind.

The bed's a mat
I rub with grass-skin.
Their sole-touches
are flute-whispers
to my beggar ears.
I lie awake—
my childhood returns
wrapped in coconut,
a naked roar
under my tongue.

Wetness is a wave
that arrives on
webbed feet.
It turns me woman,
then a midnight corpse.
My breath is a blur
against the sea.
My secrets wash water.
The doctor is a ghost
who mends socks

by night and sells
crutches by day.

I want to move.
To the rhythm
of snakes
in crowded zoos,
to the temper
of planktons
in belching seas.
I want to move
to a wayfarer's lust.
For lust comes
only in anarchy,
in a stranger's shoes.

I am poor.
My marijuana limbs
are Crusoe's island.
Nothing moves
except cannibal feet.
I wait for stranger ships,
for snail crawl,
for sparrow smoke,
for you, stranger.

Nothing moves
in my city, stranger,
nothing except lust.
For you stranger,
my legs are statues.
For you I've waited,
to make me move—
to turn me from
mountain to river,
scar to pus,
a toe-ring bell.

And you'll look away,
just, just because
I can't walk?
Because I haven't
walked through wars?
Are legs all—
carriers of hunger?
Is stillness a plague?

String dancers' eyes
on deer-tails for me,
make me ghungroos,
make me the wind
on a lantern's tongue,
a plough on land,
lightning on a flag,
dew simmering in the sun,
make me a wound,
a rotting fruit
that moves as it dies.
Stranger,
make me a lie,
make me your heart,
make me move,
make me your lust.

Sadness

Sadness is a white crane on a white cow.
Only one can bear the weight of another.

Sadness is white sand on a river bank.
It is white even when wet.

Sadness is white hibiscus resting on a fence.
It has a white bud and a white corpse.

Sadness is a snow-covered tree, eyelashes of white.
Its branches droop with its own weight.

Sadness is a wild elephant's tusk, sharp, a deposition of years.
It has beauty and grace only from a distance.

Sadness is the sclera, the screen from which hurt drips.
It washes itself, tinges red and becomes white again.

Sadness is a museum, pictures on white walls.
You leave it but it never leaves you.

Second Language

Who does not know another language does not know his own.
—Goethe

My Nephew Grows into Verbs

i.
Is

Even curiosity demands ceremony.
The three-year-old's voice is a ripe fruit thudding to the ground.
On the wall are spit marks, coloured rust by betel leaf.
For him these could be photographs on walls.
The human form is not a standard design—
everything doesn't need a face.
Time is damp. It'll soak him into agedness.
Running water is wildlife to him.
Anger has loose innards.
The horizon is a monkey.
Emotion has fingers.
Danger is a stimulant.
Everything is a sculpture.
And happiness is a piece of coincidence.

ii.
Be

An aunt's love is always tropical.
There is extravagant moisture in that affection.
My nephew wants to see love as if it were a thing—
breakable, malleable, chewable, and like plastic.
I want to tell him that transparency is overrated,
that it can't hold my love.
Imagine your intestines visible, I say, as you eat.
The little boy can't. And so he asks for a glass of water.
Nothing happens in the mirror, he withdraws.
I know he's looking for architecture,
for a building that will lock away all affection,
that which doesn't let him fall or pull him to bed at nine.
For affection is like gravity—
it holds without chains.

iii.
Am

My nephew overestimates the intelligence of water.
He wishes that the wind was prettier.
Smell is an enemy that he'll tame soon.
Heat he treats, rightly, as competition.
Light is his parents' religion.
The tongue is a Lego toy building—
it'll collapse if too much is piled on it.
He still can't grasp the hangover caused by books.
The window is a camera with a perennially open aperture.
The bed is a roadless park.
And life is as temporary as a ladder.

My nephew grows into Verbs.

Mirik: Travelling with Uncommon Nouns

i.
Horse

From atop a horse, the world is an abacus—
some calculation must be afoot.
But there's no *tawg-bawg-tawg-bawg* of horse hooves—
suddenly my childhood and its sounds seem like a lie.
My nephew, still a thing of wonder to himself,
non-existent until eighteen months ago,
rides the horse like an ant moving on a slipper.

The land, the road, the earth beneath our hooves,
have lost their elasticity. We fail exams in falling.
I worry about my nephew more than the horse.
I feel guilty, always my afterthought disease.

The afternoon yawns with our burden.

Calibrations of boredom differ:
this unnecessary newness, of a world on a horse,
bores me. I miss the dependence on my feet,
history repeating itself with every step.
Spring is such a season of waste.

My nephew is yet to discover boredom.
For him the world is a diaper soaked in nouns.
Mother. Father. Water. Bird.
Boredom would be a thing he'd want to touch.
To find out whether it would make him wet.

When evening comes suddenly, like an arriviste gateman
closing a park for the day, my nephew points to the sky
and tries to pull it close, like he pulls at his mother's hair.

The horse stops his trot. But my nephew doesn't want to leave.

Four legs can only carry the day. The night comes without feet.

ii.
Child

I see my brother in him, the man as boy,
and the zoom on my camera tells me
why we love miniature versions of ourselves—
dolls, children and gods.

Childhood is a tourist site with free gate passes.
You lose your ticket and can't ever leave.
By the Sumendu Lake, my nephew becomes Midas—
childhood, its spectacle a ceaseless wonder,
turns us into statues. We become labourers to his joy.
As the coolies and workers must have been to
the Chief Minister of Bengal, S.S. Ray,
he who ordered the lake to squat.

To imagine an adult as child demands a somersault of time.
Who'd have guessed that my mother was an infant,
her feet a thing of wonder thrown up to the sky?
Now she evens out creases on paper napkins like a maniac.

Once there was no lake here, nothing except marshland.
Men come for water now, and mountains, and conifers.
These are the new gods—on holidays, men are converts,
changing into happier versions of themselves.
For that is the tourist's aim—the Himalayas as shrink chamber.
The banks of the lake are a giant couch
on which men lie down for mass therapy.
It's hypnotism, this ambition hidden inside a holiday 'package',
this desire to escape that turns every idiom a prison—
salaries, marriages, kitchens, adulthood.

My nephew knows none of these.
The shorthand for life has come to him early.
He slaps the loose sand to watch it fly.
Everything should move in his kingdom.
And so the shortened lifespan
of television sets, taps, things with wheels.

By the lake in Mirik, everything is still that Sunday,
even the air over the pink candyfloss.
Only my mother's eyebrows move occasionally.

And my nephew.
He is the day's comet, the obedient sand following him his tail.
When he falls asleep, we fold the day like clothes for ironing.
The sky suddenly spits out its light.
Back in the hotel, we tear the night's price-tag.

iii.
Lake

My nephew doesn't know the amour in water yet.
He only cares for wetness that doesn't hurt.
Sumendu Lake is no different from his drool.
Or the tears he's observing on a young woman's cheeks.
She's a lover—that is all that matters on this April day by the water.
Beside her is her lover, his past karma in the wet hankie in her hand.

My nephew trots closer to watch them—
as if they were incarnations of water. Or the lake.
They ignore him. He could be a tree, a bird, the moon:
a child is like them all, with no understanding.

My nephew doesn't yet know that the world is an outsider.
His life has been all inside, a centripetal flow of milk and images.
Curiosity is his religion, he a new convert.
By the lake, he turns missionary.
He touches the young woman's right cheek.

Water is his reward. He is happy. The woman smiles.
Her loves approves—a child subsidising his woman's tears.
The man looks for a return gift. Nothing catches his eyes.
Not until my nephew, suddenly adult in his intuition,
points to the lake. On it is a yellow boat without men.

'I wish I could give you the lake,' he tells my nephew, his Nepali a forlorn music. The woman is sad again. The lake had never been offered to her, she thinks. The tip of her umbrella touches the skin of the water.

The Lexicographer in Lower Assam

There is a dictionary of light, the age-bent man tells me.
The shadows of his fingers are licking the wall.
He's abandoned them. Once they kidnapped his mind.
'Meaning must have a permanent shape;
You can't trust shadows.'
I ask him about the Kamtapuri dictionary he's compiled.
He looks at my shadow and begins speaking to it.
Meaning is always elsewhere.
I look to my left, and then behind, where my shadow is relaxing.

Because language must be like wine—old, aged, ancient—
he brings out the birth certificate of his mother tongue.
Kamtapuri, sixteenth century, language, conqueror—
the words acquire girth in the dimly lit room.
A kerosene lamp burns. That light's pension is richer
than the man and his language. And mine.

I don't need an interpreter,
I say to the man who's brought me here.
Our shadows stand in a queue
like I imagine meanings do in a dictionary.

A sharp wind bursts into the room.
We sneeze, the man and I, and then the light.
Betel nuts and betel leaves arrive for guests.
Relationships must begin from the mouth.

Dictionaries are fat books, heavy to lift to the eye.
How could their compiler be so thin?
'I have put *my* entire life here,' he says.
My mind is diuretic—
Where is the subjectivity in dictionaries?
'Everyone should know at least two languages,' he says.
I grow nervous. I'm scared of meeting meaning half-way.

'Light,' he says, pointing to the lamp, the wick eating itself,
and then stands in front of it, 'Darkness'.
Meaning must come from comparison, he demonstrates.

The first volume is out already, the third is in his almirah.
It's the second that is lost, he says. I look away from the tears.
That publisher has stolen it, he concludes.
Curses about darkness follow. I adjust my spine.
But light is both host and guest. I am too tired to debate.
What could a stolen dictionary *mean*?

We are a friendly people, he affirms. His shadow touches mine.
His grandson opens a black umbrella in front of the lamp.
A schoolgirl is learning her lessons:
'Sunlight comes to Assam before the rest of India...'

'Is a dictionary a *natural* thing?' I ask.
Exhaustion's given my voice a late accent.
He stands up. Anger's a new immigrant in his voice.
'A dictionary is the most hospitable place in the world.
Where else would the foreign find such accommodation?'

When I get up from my wicker chair to leave,
the hoarder of words turns me into a policeman—
'Please help me to find my stolen dictionary.'

At the gate, he adjusts the hair on my forehead.
'In a dictionary nothing can be out of place.'

Spit Feast

We come to sea from air to feast,
to sink and stub all prepositions.
Thhoo. We come to sea for soliloquy.
Thhoo. One speaker, one water, one love.
Thhoo. Blood makes its own demands:
heat, flow, clot, and the need
to conquer numbers. *Thhoo.*

To look at the sea—to believe in it—
is to know that there is nothing beyond it.
Thhoo. We come to sea to spit,
to hiss without reserve,
to become ululation. *Thhoo.*
Here, in the sea, is our spit's
final destination. *Thhoo.*

We come to sea to drown witches,
those oversexed beasts
that live in our winter clocks:
boredom, impatience, deadlines.
Thhoo. To look at the waves is to discover
how the sea serves tirelessness,
the ancient god of love. *Thhoo.*
For only love is more tireless than the sea.

Like an infant playing with its legs,
the sea entertains itself. Its rest
is always the sand. There the *thhoo.*
We come to sea to stop being man.
For only humans spit after a feast. *Thhoo.*

We come to sea to be assured
that our spit will reach the other.
Thhoo. We come to sea to encounter
what we have feared most:
the privacy of spit in our marriage.
Thhoo. Here our feet can touch,
as the roots of our lives do,
without the entanglement of mouths.
Thhoo. Our hands, our leaves, our nails
remain, eager with penitence,
but scared to touch. *Thhoo.*

And then, as sea-sand soaks spit,
and our tongues tire of feasts,
we preserve histories like dentures.
The mouth's vengeance in a jar: *Thhoo.*

'Go to Pakistan'

There was always the regret of being born after the birth of proverbs,
of being an arriviste when a teacher said 'Too many cooks spoil
 the broth.'
For in your home was only one cook, a tired and reluctant mother
 de-seeding papayas.
Or when your grandfather behaved like god, saying, 'Honesty is the
 best policy.'
You wanted to tell him how that adage had passed its expiry date.
What silliness might have incubated that folk knowledge, what
 strange times?
No history book tells you those; historians don't care for the
 birthdates of wisdom.

You've known it intuitively, how every generation gives birth to at
 least one.
You laugh at those that fuelled your parents: 'Aaram Haram Hai.'
They owe their knee pains and life insurance policies to it.
You laugh at your uncle, who was nearly killed by 'Indira Hatao,
 Desh Bachao.'
One day you suddenly notice how aphorisms are always by the
 anonymous.
And you immediately turn into an adult. You grow anxious, you
 are a competitor.
You want your generation's proverb to be victorious, as if wisdom
 were a bestselling category.
You still don't understand the difference between proverbs and
 slogans.
You can't yet see the scaffolding of history that keeps slogans alive.
Proverbs are a community's heirlooms—you must measure your
 height against them.

Your stadium sports grow shorter: playtime the distance between home and the workplace.
Your eyes feed industries and capitalism—everything is an advert, including yourself.
Your generation still hasn't found a proverb.
You wonder whether it's a-one-word magic: 'Delete'.
You vote like you get married: in both you are tourists. The serious leaves you aimless.
Silence is too domestic, a stupor. You turn to the noise for a proverb.
The clamour and the anger have scanned the statement:
'Go to Pakistan.'
At first it surprises you, its teenage parody of 'Go to Hell.'
Then you feel it grow inside you, like a male hormone, pushing your skin, giving you pleasure.

An actor says something on TV. He is only describing the shape of his fear.
They give it definition. He's made a film called *Ra.One*. And *Don*.
A Yogi turns him into a terrorist. 'Go to Pakistan'. Chuck De India.
It could be a film, the dialogues thrown at him:
He lives here but his 'aatma is in Pakistan'.
But this aatma is not soul, it's the colloquial for ghost.
Pakistan becomes a graveyard story.

It's been growing through the summer, the words gathering girth.
You still can't find the moral in the adage.
The Bandra police beat up the Shaikh brothers and instruct, 'Go to Pakistan'.
'*Those who are dying without beef can go to Pakistan.*'
'*If Muslims want any special treatment as Muslims, they should go to Pakistan.*'
'*Those opposed to Narendra Modi should go to Pakistan.*'
'*If the BJP loses in Bihar, crackers will burst in Pakistan.*'
'*Say "Vande Mataram" or go to Pakistan.*'
Pakistan—Slaughter House, Luxury Spa, Language School.
They become travel agents—Sell That Place, Send Them to Pakistan.

Sometimes they want to break the monotony. They make it sound like 'Kaala Pani'.
Ghulam Ali will sing in Delhi. They are insecure, they change the verb.
'Go' invites its opposite: Don't you dare come here; Stay in Pakistan.
And everyday new Partitions grow inside televisions.
One day, a crow flies away with an ear of baby corn.
The young greengrocer's words pursue the bird: 'Go to Pakistan.'
And you grow certain that this is how all proverbs are born.

Sounds

i.
'I love you'

You dislike the tourism in the words but you let them remain,
like a nose that one needs for breathing, whatever its shape.
Do you change the font when I say them to you?
Is it its speed you dislike, its lack of revelation, its costumeness?
I imagine you tell me that these words are all mouth,
too open, like a martyr's body, that you prefer love with eyelids,
that let light in and disappear. But you say nothing,
not these words which I wait for, as if saying them
would make a doll lose its heritage. You give these words
humour, their rust and grease. 'I love you,' I say, like one in exile.
The words are in disrepair. 'I know,' you say in response.
I feel like a thief who doesn't know the worth of his loot.
'I love you,' I say again, as if I was learning a new language.
I hear your tendrilled smile: 'Are you sure?' you say, teasing.
And the three words turn into news—a weather report.

ii.
'Idiot'

'Idiot.' We do not call each other by name,
as if the world was a wind that'd break the bones in our names.
'Idiot.' That's like our connubial word, a glue, a game.
Passing the parcel. 'Idiot.'
More joyous, more full of playful conviction than 'I will.'
'Idiot.' Its sound as dense as ritual, naked as laughter.
It's the word's stockiness we love—how it gives our love its vowels.
'Idiot.' This is our sacred secret, our soft slap,
how it turns us metal, makes us buckle as if it were heat.
The word changes alkalinity as it travels between us—
we ferry the word's instinct, we allow it drama.
'Idiot.' This grace note, as pure as a gambler's wish.

It returns—'Idiot'; 'Idiot'—like satellites.
And we come together,
like numbers—'like youth, idiot'—meld into one another,
like people—'like light, idiot'—in a photograph.

iii.
'Mmm-mah'

This is how you perform synaesthesia—turning touch to sound.
This new genre—*the kiss on the phone.*
Mmm-mah. Mmm-mah. Mmm-mah.
The line amplifies their sound; or it's my heart.
Mmm-mah. Emphatic, like a rubber stamp.
And yet not one is a replica of the other,
each as different as the waves in a sea.
And each like the wave that I know will return to me.
Like sleep does every night, new and old, like fresh clothes.
At night, when all thoughts gather as if darkness were a station,
I am suddenly jealous of the phone, and soon of the air,
where the wireless is, where all your kisses are.
I'm nervous, I'm possessive.
What if they drop from the sky on someone else?
Later, in the stickiness of my dreams, I'm a trapeze artist,
my trail a crowd of your kisses in the air.
'Mmm-mah,' you say again, that sound purer than 'kiss'.
The eloquence of those who give is full of moist stains.

iv.
'Dhyateriki'

'Dhyateriki.' That sound even before my admiration has uncurled.
I'm talking, my words like cutlery, making sounds as they hit you.
The sound of your happy shyness—'Dhyateriki'—
its syllables like an East European surname.
Its provincial lilt, and its comedy, condensed into its diminutive,
like an annotation—your 'Dhyat'—in this thing so rare:
a woman describing her man's body.

There is no grammar here, no readymade metaphor.
The perfection of your form, the disorder in my glands,
skin the colour of late dawn, shoulder blades as robust as eagerness.
This encounter with beauty at eye level, this intimacy with form.
Form? My words don't form—they forget to grow up, they honk.
'Looking at your beauty one becomes aware of its inequality.'
I want to say something more, but you stop me. 'Dhyateriki.'

v.
Silence

Every relationship must have its neologism.
This is ours—silence on the phone,
which we strain to hear more attentively than words.
It is not the glamour of silence we seek but its foreplay,
a ventilator that keeps everything in suspense,
as if love were a risk, only an excitement.
We are arguing without words, we who love their theatre.
We are children, waiting for the other to speak first—
say anything; like breaking the folds of ironed clothes.
We are restless—the horizon of this silence seems too far away.

Only the surface catches light. And so with silence.
We know it's inside us—a word, and the silence will be cured.
'Hello,' we say together, suddenly, as if it were an antibiotic.
And then the love begins, again, our love, as endless as silence.

Botany

*'Comparing seeds. Trying experiments
in salting them to see if they'd survive
floating across an ocean.'
To, for instance, the Galapagos.
'Have begun, at last, my species book. Shall call it
Natural Selection.'*

—Ruth Padel

The Afterlife of Trees and Their Lovers

i.
Jagadish Chandra Bose's house, Mayapuri, Darjeeling

I have come here to learn a foreign language—
plants must have a mother tongue?
To the aborigines, the words for tree and house were the same.
And so this mountain house of Jagadish Chandra Bose.
It is easy to turn this into a folk tale,
to see the scientist reincarnated as a tree.
Like the seven brothers Champa?
But they were tortured; not Bose.
It is difficult to imagine a history of trees
without man in it. Man as tree, Tree as tale.

At Lloyd's Botanical Garden in Darjeeling,
I look for immigrants, plants who travelled well,
those that might have been Bose's muse—
'Plants are living things', the thought now textbook aphorism.
On my way uphill is the sacrifice of grass, the silence of soil.
Sometimes a different time zone—flowers are late risers.

I think of myths—
the forgetfulness of scientists,
jackfruit children, like Jamini Roy's 'mother and child',
gechho bhoot, ghosts of Bengali trees,
the absent-mindedness of seasonal plants.
Do these conifers remember Bose?
Or the moss on walls, the punishment for waiting?

In Bose's sparse living room, the window is a mirror.
Cleanliness has done it great violence,
the grass is now green only on the other side.
Not a pot or vase in the wooden house.
I choke on my surprise—a crematorium grows inside me.
Botany is only a history of the personality of plants.

ii.
Shakti Chattopadhyay's house, Baharu, South 24 Parganas

'Are you General or Scheduled Caste?'
This is a question put to a betel nut tree in Baharu.
Shakti Chattopadhyay might have asked that question,
but would he inscribe it on the tree trunk like an insecure lover,
making the bark a government census roll?

Instead of Shakti's green room, I see red—
the soil's blood congealed into the orange flowers of Krishnachura,
the tree a leech sucking the earth's haemoglobin.
The fields in Baharu are a morgue every morning;
the sweeper deposits flower corpses in the earth's mass coffin.

Near Shakti's old house, the leaves move like flags,
like a bad mood, against the direction of thought.
Shakti knew the xenophobia caused by trees
in human spaces—beds, buses, bathrooms.
I suddenly spot trees that look suicidal,
those that Shakti might have scolded.
'Does the garden know every plant in it?'
he asked in that famous poem, you remember?

As I board the bus, I think of life insurance policies
that the drunken poet might have bought for these trees.
Later, in the parks, I only see decapitated shrubs,
green Kanishkas standing on bulldozed grass.
Every tree is a folk tale.
Only some shed their morals like leaves.

iii.
Bodhi Tree, Bodh Gaya

Here you can come without brushing your teeth—
the Buddha and the fig tree have never needed toothbrushes.
The myths that surround places are like ambulance sirens—
patients, pilgrims and tourists are all the same.
One comes to trees to escape the pornography of waiting.
There must be something about sitting under a tree,
in the bandaged conflation between shade and shadow.
Other men chose exile in the forest, vanwas—
Rama, the five Pandava brothers, their wives.
Only Siddhartha came to a solitary tree, to escape desire.
A forest is a hiding place, where men compete with trees.
So Gautama stopped walking and closed his eyes.
The uselessness of eyes, of legs, of combs, of words—
all this the Buddha learned from this tree.

Today, only bombs are living Buddhas.
When one went off in Gaya, everyone ran,
everyone except the trees.
For death also demands walking.
Now, after the fret of flowering,
I only seek the tree's heart.
Guns are seedless fruits,
the gardens full of traitor trees.
Now I am free.
Only I know that the tree is Buddha.
And that the Buddha was a tree.

Art

*Others have seen what is and asked why.
I have seen what could be and asked why not.*
—Pablo Picasso

Portraits: Shards

i.
Rear-view Mirror

Portraits, too, are criticism.
But they cannot ask you for forgiveness.
You wipe the dust off your smile.
And a stop-gap peace is made.
Self-love is the only constant.
All other loves are temporary.
You are so poor that you have no memories.
But there are also some who own nothing
except the wind in their hair.

ii.
Window Pane

There is a militancy in domesticity
that you recognise only after opening a window.
Dusty surfaces make for awkward canvases—
marks of soap water create leftover worry lines,
fame has its own anxiety, its blood rises to the eyebrow.
Portraits here are self-vigilance. You are you plus one.
On a window pane, portraits are fitness certificates
in a foreign language.

iii.
Dead Screen

You pity the blind for being deprived of these everyday portraits.
You want to tell them that we all look the same—
those with eyes and those without.
That these dead screens of televisions, computers, phones
hold on them only judgment, not insight.
That the movement of hair is always against the gradient of
    civilisation.

iv.
Car Window

That fog is a function of light
comes to you only when the back of your mirror dies.
Not old mercury but water's afterlife.
Portraits behave like automobiles,
dropping unnecessary occupants on the way.
This car window, with its moving portraits,
has not known the violence of unreciprocated love.
When it rains, the portraits become water carriers.
And you feel the joyous burden of a child carrying rain in his pockets.

v.
Skype Window

Love comes like news.
Distance nurtures ambition.
Your Skype image grows larger each day.
Domestic life moves behind you like a halo.
Its large-heartedness surprises you,
this portrait as accommodative as your diary.
After the high-pitched talk and the low light,
you walk out of your portrait with second-hand description—
someone said you have 'tribal shoulders'.
Outside, there is life and there is untimely sleep.
Sunlight feeds on your eyes like meat.
Sleep grazes on it like a cow.

vi.
Coffee Cup Reflection

Here you are as smooth as baby food.
Happiness pickles into grief when left unstirred.
You wish for your talent to reflect in portraits.
Instead, there is the uncertainty about bad angles.
Beauty is always a prisoner—

it grows rebellious inside the cup, fumes into steam.
You adjust your hair but nothing changes.
The irrelevance of beauty makes you think of love as middleaged.
And lovers as intrusive mountaineers.

vii.
Spoon Face

There are more poems about the moon than wives.
Love wants to domesticate everything—
even sleep and sunlight.
Your face on the spoon is outside the curriculum.
And so every profile is a mistake, a failed mark.
You are grateful for this portrait's short life.
Every face must find a spoon, every flower a spade.

viii.
X-ray Plate

In front of you is your twin, the other half of an argument.
(Illness is also your portrait—
Think of the indisciplined lines of an ECG
testing your heart's endurance.)
The destiny of your bones, like bricks, to stand,
gives your portrait the grace of a curtain.
This portrait of your insides is silent music,
related to you only like lust is to gravity.

ix.
Blood-stained Paper

When blood soaks into passive paper,
you wonder whether the paper is like you—
a non-vegetarian.
Your portrait is a leech.
A thing in eclipse is also a complete thing.
And so this sanitary napkin, this bloodied map.
Portraits are like the night—they accumulate bodies in parts.

x.
Death Mask

Life has been a harvest of waste.
Your death mask is a late moral,
your last portrait, a rhetoric of loss.
But metaphor is never private.
Death is too mainstream—
you've avoided it thus far.
You see it coming now, like a step-lover,
turning you into a duck, with wings that cannot fly.
This last portrait is a history of tiredness.

www.ingramcontent.com/pod-product-compliance
Lightning Source LLC
Chambersburg PA
CBHW052052220426
43663CB00012B/2541